EP Physics/Chemistry Printables: Levels 1-4

This book belongs to:

_____

This book was made for your convenience. It is available for printing from the Easy Peasy All-in-One Homeschool website. It contains all of the printables from Easy Peasy's physics/chemistry course. The instructions for each page are found in the online course.

Easy Peasy All-in-One Homeschool is a free online homeschool curriculum providing high quality education for children around the globe. It provides complete courses for preschool through high school graduation. For EP's curriculum visit allinonehomeschool.com.

EP Physics/Chemistry Printables: Levels 1-4

This workbook, made by Tina Rutherford with permission from Easy Peasy All-in-One Homeschool, is based on the physics/chemistry component of Easy Peasy's curriculum. For EP's online curriculum visit allinonehomeschool.com.

ISBN: 9781096808183

First Edition: August 2019

Element Lapbook
Pages

Cut along the outside lines and fold in half. Write the name of the element and information about the element inside the booklet.

Glue this side to the correct periodic table group section.

H

1

Cut along the outside lines and fold in half. Write the name of the element and information about the element inside the booklet.

Glue this side to the correct periodic table group section.

He

2

Cut along the outside lines and fold in half. Write the name of the element and information about the element inside the booklet.

Glue this side to the correct periodic table group section.

C

6

| Cut along the outside lines and fold in half. Write the name of the element and information about the element inside the booklet.

Glue this side to the correct periodic table group section. | O

8 |

| Cut along the outside lines and fold in half. Write the name of the element and information about the element inside the booklet.

Glue this side to the correct periodic table group section. | Ne

10 |

| Cut along the outside lines and fold in half. Write the name of the element and information about the element inside the booklet.

Glue this side to the correct periodic table group section. | Na

11 |

Cut along the outside lines and fold in half. Write the name of the element and information about the element inside the booklet.

Glue this side to the correct periodic table group section.

Mg

12

Cut along the outside lines and fold in half. Write the name of the element and information about the element inside the booklet.

Glue this side to the correct periodic table group section.

Al

13

Cut along the outside lines and fold in half. Write the name of the element and information about the element inside the booklet.

Glue this side to the correct periodic table group section.

Si

14

Cut along the outside lines and fold in half. Write the name of the element and information about the element inside the booklet.

Glue this side to the correct periodic table group section.

Cl

17

Cut along the outside lines and fold in half. Write the name of the element and information about the element inside the booklet.

Glue this side to the correct periodic table group section.

K

19

Cut along the outside lines and fold in half. Write the name of the element and information about the element inside the booklet.

Glue this side to the correct periodic table group section.

20

Cut along the outside lines and fold in half. Write the name of the element and information about the element inside the booklet. Glue this side to the correct periodic table group section.	Fe 26

Cut along the outside lines and fold in half. Write the name of the element and information about the element inside the booklet. Glue this side to the correct periodic table group section.	Ni 28

Cut along the outside lines and fold in half. Write the name of the element and information about the element inside the booklet. Glue this side to the correct periodic table group section.	Cu 29

Cut along the outside lines and fold in half. Write the name of the element and information about the element inside the booklet.

Glue this side to the correct periodic table group section.

Zn

30

Cut along the outside lines and fold in half. Write the name of the element and information about the element inside the booklet.

Glue this side to the correct periodic table group section.

47

Cut along the outside lines and fold in half. Write the name of the element and information about the element inside the booklet.

Glue this side to the correct periodic table group section.

18

Cut along the outside lines and fold in half. Write the name of the element and information about the element inside the booklet.

Glue this side to the correct periodic table group section.

I

53

Cut along the outside lines and fold in half. Write the name of the element and information about the element inside the booklet.

Glue this side to the correct periodic table group section.

Au

79

Cut along the outside lines and fold in half. Write the name of the element and information about the element inside the booklet.

Glue this side to the correct periodic table group section.

Pb

82

Periodic Table of the Elements

Group→	1	2	3	4	5	6	7	8	9	10	11	12	13	14	15	16	17	18
↓Period																		
1	1 H																	2 He
2	3 Li	4 Be											5 B	6 C	7 N	8 O	9 F	10 Ne
3	11 Na	12 Mg											13 Al	14 Si	15 P	16 S	17 Cl	18 Ar
4	19 K	20 Ca	21 Sc	22 Ti	23 V	24 Cr	25 Mn	26 Fe	27 Co	28 Ni	29 Cu	30 Zn	31 Ga	32 Ge	33 As	34 Se	35 Br	36 Kr
5	37 Rb	38 Sr	39 Y	40 Zr	41 Nb	42 Mo	43 Tc	44 Ru	45 Rh	46 Pd	47 Ag	48 Cd	49 In	50 Sn	51 Sb	52 Te	53 I	54 Xe
6	55 Cs	56 Ba		72 Hf	73 Ta	74 W	75 Re	76 Os	77 Ir	78 Pt	79 Au	80 Hg	81 Tl	82 Pb	83 Bi	84 Po	85 At	86 Rn
7	87 Fr	88 Ra		104 Rf	105 Db	106 Sg	107 Bh	108 Hs	109 Mt	110 Ds	111 Rg	112 Cn	113 Uut	114 Fl	115 Uup	116 Lv	117 Uus	118 Uuo

Lanthanides	57 La	58 Ce	59 Pr	60 Nd	61 Pm	62 Sm	63 Eu	64 Gd	65 Tb	66 Dy	67 Ho	68 Er	69 Tm	70 Yb	71 Lu
Actinides	89 Ac	90 Th	91 Pa	92 U	93 Np	94 Pu	95 Am	96 Cm	97 Bk	98 Cf	99 Es	100 Fm	101 Md	102 No	103 Lr

Worksheet Pages

Solids, Liquids, Gasses

Write in each box whether the indicated picture represents a solid, liquid, or gas.

rain
liquid

sky
gas

basket
solid

hot air
gas

lemon
solid

air
gas

ice
solid

lemonade
liquid

pot
solid

steam
gas

water
liquid

Experiment Worksheet

Fill out this worksheet as you work through the experiment.

Question: _Will a sound travel better through a_
liquid or gas

Hypothesis: _____
_____

Materials: _Spoon F_____
_____

Procedure: _tie 2ft string to a spoon & hit it_
on the table
_____
_____
_____

Observations/data: _____
_____
_____
_____
_____

Conclusion: _____
_____
_____

Reflecting Light

Draw arrows representing light waves to show how the bear can see the book and the boy can see the key.

Draw arrows representing light waves to show how the boy and girl can see their respective flashlight beams. The rectangle objects are mirrors.

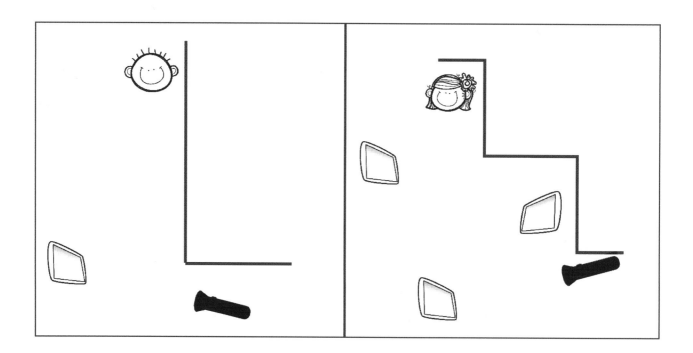

Experiment Worksheet

Fill out this worksheet as you work through the experiment.

Question: _____

Hypothesis: _____
_____

Materials: _____
_____

Procedure: _____
_____
_____
_____
_____

Observations/data: _____
_____
_____
_____

Conclusion: _____
_____
_____

Atoms

Label the parts of the atom. Then use the bottom of the page to draw a hydrogen atom. A hydrogen atom has one proton and one electron with zero neutrons.

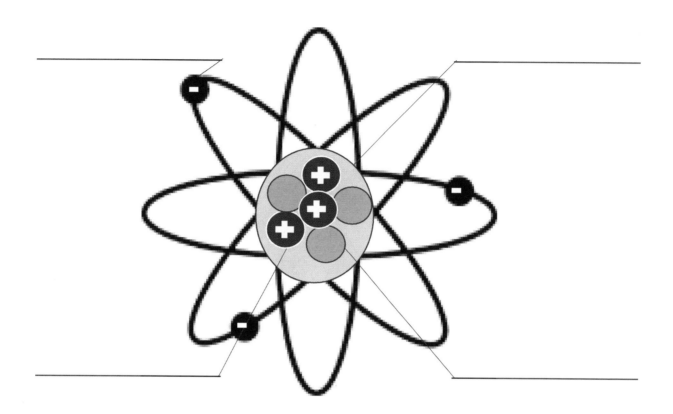

Hydrogen Atom:

Chemical Reaction

Use this notebooking page to write a simple definition of a chemical reaction.

_____

_____

_____

_____

_____

Aeronautics

Answer the question, "What is aeronautics?"

_____

_____

_____

_____

_____

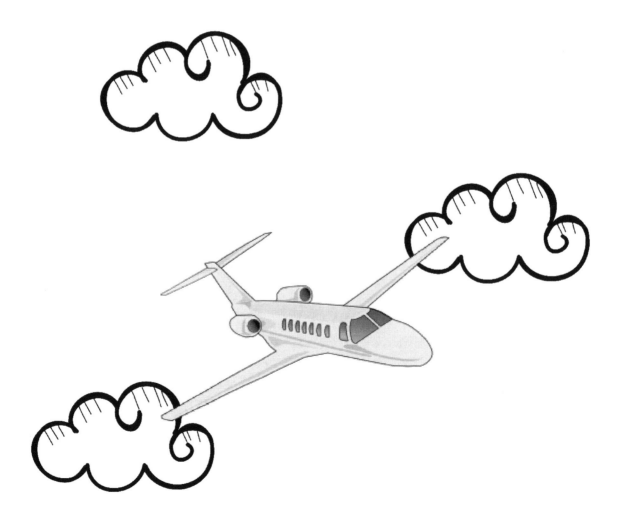

Flight Forces

Cut out these labels and tape them onto the string and straw.

thrust

drag

lift

weight

Weight on Other Planets

The surface gravity of each planet relative to earth is in its box. Find out your weight on other planets by writing your weight on earth on the line and multiplying it by the surface gravity of the planet.

Mercury	Venus	Earth
_____	_____	_____
x .38	x .91	x 1

Mars	Jupiter	Saturn
_____	_____	_____
x .38	x 2.36	x 1.05

Uranus	Neptune	Pluto
_____	_____	_____
x .94	x 1.13	x .07

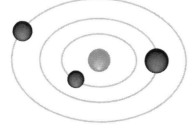

Rotor Motor

Use this template to make your rotor motor. Cut on the solid lines and fold on the dotted lines. Fold A and B in opposite directions, fold X and Y toward the center, and fold Z up for rigidity.

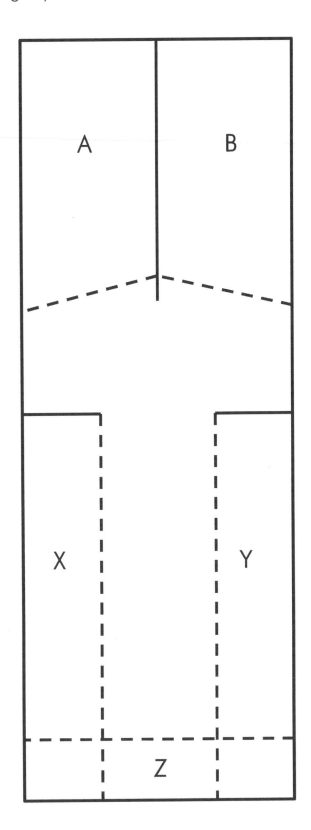

Acid Test

Use this sheet to record your findings.

Objective: to find if something is an acid by observing its reaction to baking soda

Testing	Produces gas?	Other observations
Vinegar	yes	

pH Test

Use this sheet to record your findings.

Objective: to find out if liquids are acid, neutral, or base

Testing	Color	Conclusion
Vinegar	pink	acid

Acids and Bases

Answer the following questions about acids and bases.

What is a characteristic of an acid? _____

_____

What is a characteristic of a base? _____

_____

List some acids: _____

List some bases: _____

What is the pH of a strong acid? _____

What color does a strong acid turn when tested for its pH
level? _____

What is the pH of a strong base? _____

What color does a strong base turn when tested for its pH
level? _____

Knotted Bones

Draw a picture of your chicken bone as it looks now and then answer the questions.

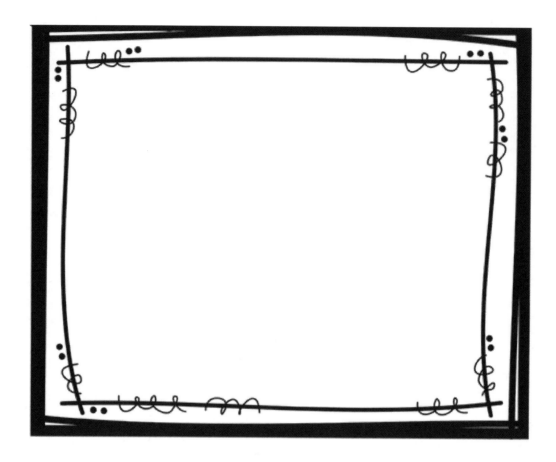

What I saw: _____

_____

_____

_____

What I did: _____

_____

_____

_____

Buoyancy Test

Use this sheet to record your findings.

Objective: to find out if objects are buoyant or not.

Testing	Buoyant	Not Buoyant
rock		X

Properties of Water

Draw pictures of the following terms.

Viscosity

Density

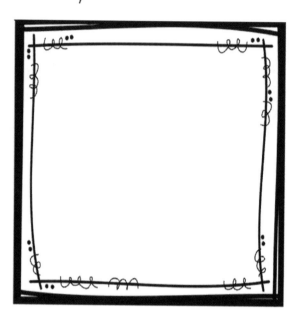

Buoyancy

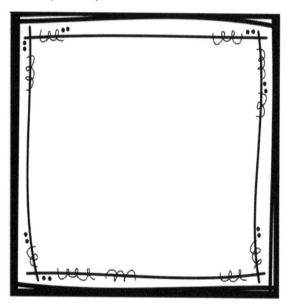

Capillary Action

Electricity Timeline

Use the blanks to fill in a timeline of electricity events you want to remember. Be sure to include the year.

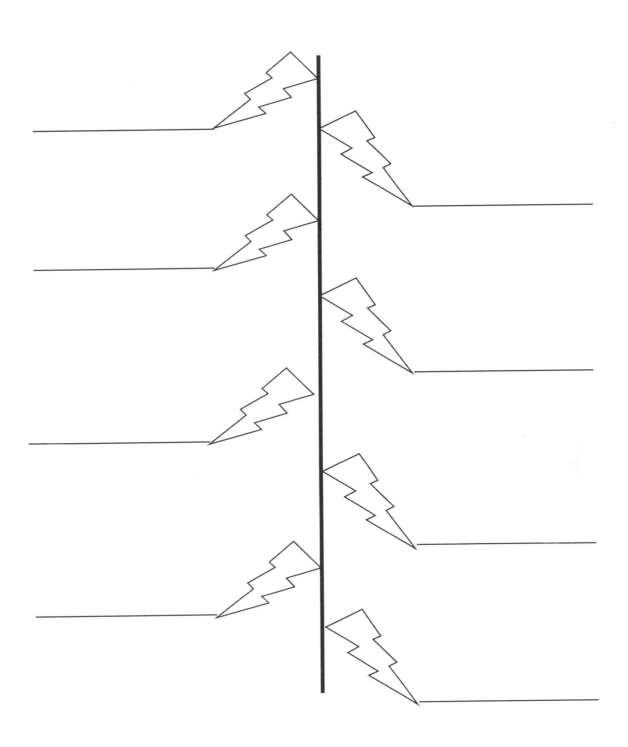

Circuits

Record observations from your experiment.

_____

_____

_____

Color in the light bulb that would turn on in the two circuits below. One is a closed circuit, and one is an open circuit. Can you label them?

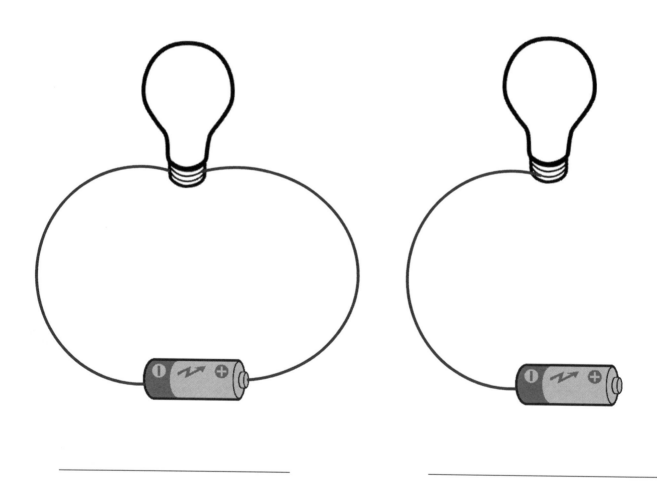

_____   _____

Types of Electricity

Use this page to define the terms.

electricity_____

_____

_____

static electricity_____

_____

_____

current electricity_____

_____

_____

Famous Electricians

What did each of the following people contribute to the field of electricity?

Thomas Edison

_____

_____

_____

Albert Einstein

_____

_____

_____

Benjamin Franklin

_____

_____

_____

Michael Faraday

_____

_____

_____

Electricity is Shocking

Why does electricity shock you?

_____

_____

_____

_____

_____

Electrical Safety

Match the scenario with the safety tip that helps you know what to do. Put the number of the tip that applies to the scenario on the line beside it. Not all tips will be used, but you should read and know them all!

1. Never climb a utility pole.

2. Never climb trees that are near powerlines.

3. Never pull a plug out by the cord.

4. Never handle taped cords, wires, or switches.

5. Only cords go into outlets.

6. Never go near a downed power line.

7. Don't stick any object into electrical equipment.

8. Never use electrical equipment around water.

9. Always ask for help if you don't understand something about electricity.

My brother says a dime will fit into the slot on my electrical outlet. Should I see if he's right? _____

My bagel is stuck in the toaster. Should I use a knife to dig it out? _____

I want to take my radio to the pool so I can listen to my favorite music. There's room on my raft for it. Should I pack it? _____

I bought a new lamp, but the old one is plugged in behind my bed and I can't reach the plug. I can reach the cord, though. Should I pull it out that way? _____

Vocabulary

Define these terms.

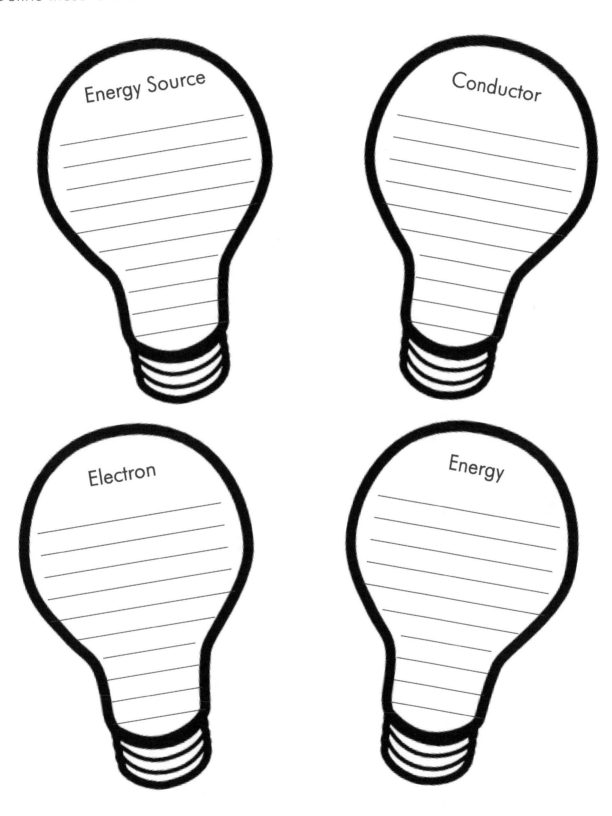

Energy Source

Conductor

Electron

Energy

Experiment Worksheet

Fill out this worksheet as you work through the experiment.

Question: _____

Hypothesis: _____

_____

Materials: _____

_____

Procedure: _____

_____

_____

_____

_____

Observations/data: _____

_____

_____

_____

_____

Conclusion: _____

_____

_____

Magnetism

What's the strongest part of a magnet?

    the poles   the middle

What's the weakest part of a magnet?

    the poles   the middle

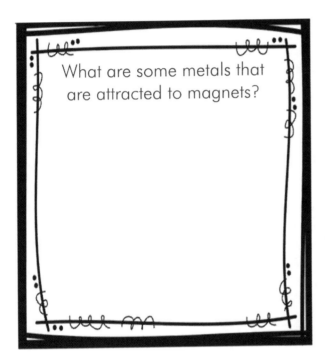

What are some metals that are attracted to magnets?

What are some metals that are not attracted to magnets?

What are some natural magnets?

_____

_____

Magnets

If you attach a bar magnet to a piece of wood and float it in water, the contraption will slowly turn until the magnet's north pole points

_____.

north   south   east   west

A popular piece of navigation equipment that uses a magnet is a

_____.

Two north poles or two south poles put together will _____ each other.

attract   repel

A south and a north pole put together will _____ each other.

attract   repel

Simple Motors

Fill in the missing words from each sentence using the word box.

alternating current	commutator	terminals	brushes

This makes the current change back and forth (much like commuting is to drive back and forth).

_____

These feed electric power.

_____

These are made from graphite or springy metal.

_____

Periodically changes direction.

_____

Label this drawing of a simple motor with the following: magnetic field, commutator, brushes, electric current. Draw an arrow in the direction the coil would rotate.

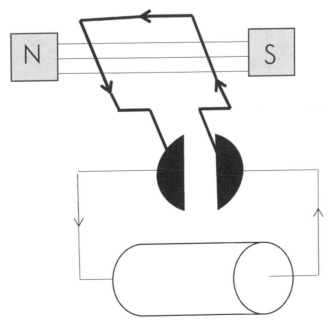

Everyday Magnets

Use this page to draw a picture of somewhere in your house where you would find a magnet. Try to think beyond the refrigerator! Share with a family member what type(s) of magnet(s) you would find in the place you drew.

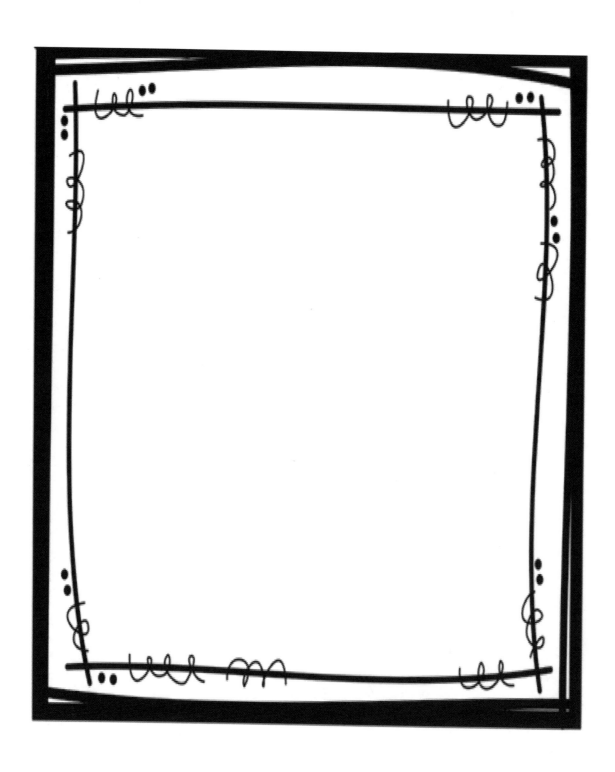

Electricity Conductors

Use this sheet to record your findings.

Objective: to find out if objects conduct or carry electricity.

Testing	Conductor	Not Conductor
water	X	

Dissolve

Use this sheet to record your findings.

Objective: to find out which substances dissolve in water.

Testing	Does it dissolve?
sugar	yes

Dissolving in Hot Water

Use this sheet to record your findings.

Objective: to find if substances dissolve the same in hot water.

Testing	Does it dissolve?	Observations
sugar	yes	

Atoms

Label the parts of the atom using the words in the box. Then use the line at the bottom to tell what type of atom it is.

| proton | neutron | electron | nucleus | orbit (shell) |

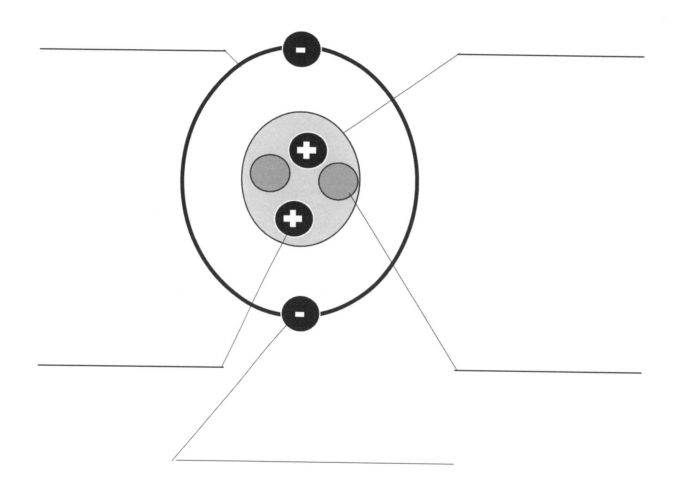

_____

Friction

Write down some examples of friction in the world around you. You can find some ideas in the pictures if you're having trouble.

	High Friction	Low Friction
Useful		
Not Useful		

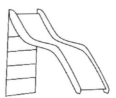

Newton's Laws of Motion

Write each of Newton's three Laws of Motion on the lines and draw a picture of an example in the boxes.

1st Law: Inertia

2nd Law: Acceleration

3rd Law: Action/Reaction

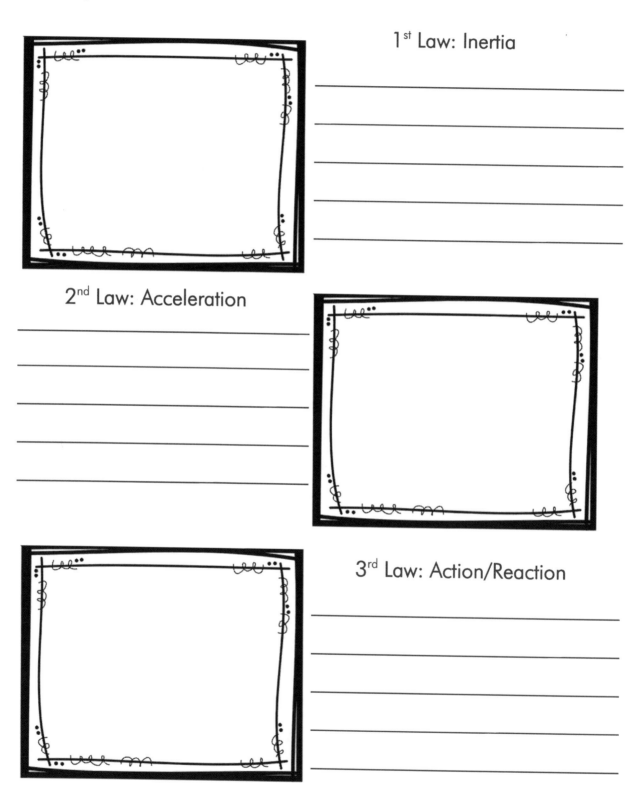

Simple Machines

Use this page to draw examples of these simple machines as they are assigned.

Inclined plane

Wedge

Lever

Screw

Wheel and axle

Pulley

Experiment Worksheet

Fill out this worksheet as you work through the experiment.

Question: _____

Hypothesis: _____

_____

Materials: _____

_____

Procedure: _____

_____

_____

_____

_____

Observations/data: _____

_____

_____

_____

_____

Conclusion: _____

_____

_____

Element Go Fish

Carefully tear out these pages and cut out the cards (there are 3 sets of 18 cards). Use them to play a game of element "Go Fish." Ask any information on the card to learn more about the elements as you play. You need 3 cards for a set.

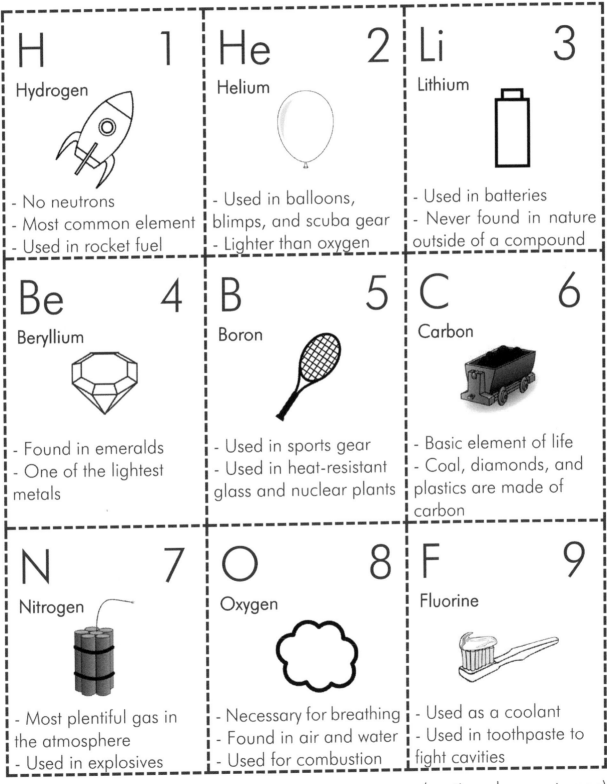

H 1 Hydrogen - No neutrons - Most common element - Used in rocket fuel	**He** 2 Helium - Used in balloons, blimps, and scuba gear - Lighter than oxygen	**Li** 3 Lithium - Used in batteries - Never found in nature outside of a compound
Be 4 Beryllium - Found in emeralds - One of the lightest metals	**B** 5 Boron - Used in sports gear - Used in heat-resistant glass and nuclear plants	**C** 6 Carbon - Basic element of life - Coal, diamonds, and plastics are made of carbon
N 7 Nitrogen - Most plentiful gas in the atmosphere - Used in explosives	**O** 8 Oxygen - Necessary for breathing - Found in air and water - Used for combustion	**F** 9 Fluorine - Used as a coolant - Used in toothpaste to fight cavities

(continued on next page)

Element Go Fish

Ne 10	Na 11	Mg 12
Neon	Sodium	Magnesium
OPEN	Salt	
- Used in lights, lasers - Never bonds to other elements	- Bonds with chlorine to make table salt - Never found alone	- Necessary for plants and animals - Found in sparklers
Al 13	**Si 14**	**P 15**
Aluminum	Silicon	Phosphorus
	ROM	
- Used in airplanes for its weight and strength - Used in foil, cables	- Found in sand, stone, and soil - Used in computer chips	- Used in matches, detergents, fertilizers - Found in bones
S 16	**Cl 17**	**Ar 18**
Sulfur	Chlorine	Argon
- Found in matches, fireworks, egg yolks - Creates air pollution	- Combines with hydrogen to digest food - Used in swimming pools	- Found in light bulbs - Does not react or bond with any other element

(continued on next page)

Element Go Fish

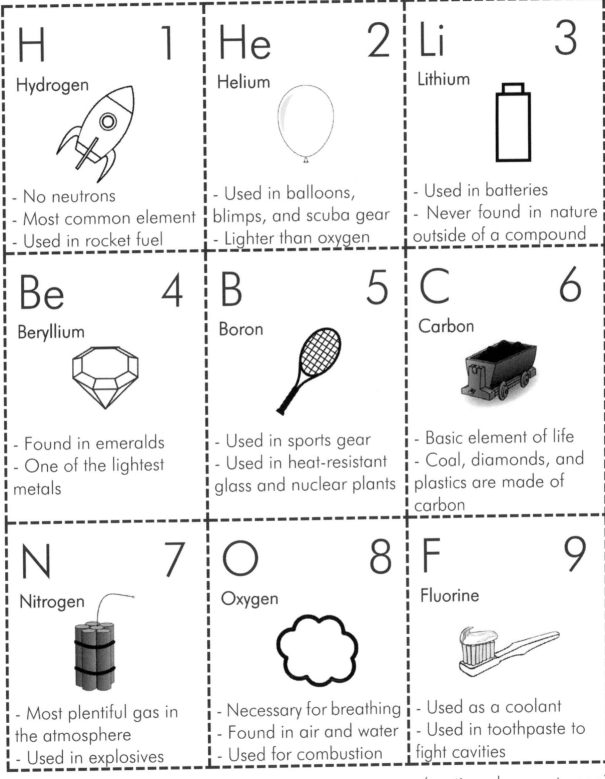

H   **1**

Hydrogen

- No neutrons
- Most common element
- Used in rocket fuel

He   **2**

Helium

- Used in balloons, blimps, and scuba gear
- Lighter than oxygen

Li   **3**

Lithium

- Used in batteries
- Never found in nature outside of a compound

Be   **4**

Beryllium

- Found in emeralds
- One of the lightest metals

B   **5**

Boron

- Used in sports gear
- Used in heat-resistant glass and nuclear plants

C   **6**

Carbon

- Basic element of life
- Coal, diamonds, and plastics are made of carbon

N   **7**

Nitrogen

- Most plentiful gas in the atmosphere
- Used in explosives

O   **8**

Oxygen

- Necessary for breathing
- Found in air and water
- Used for combustion

F   **9**

Fluorine

- Used as a coolant
- Used in toothpaste to fight cavities

(continued on next page)

Element Go Fish

Ne 10
Neon

OPEN

- Used in lights, lasers
- Never bonds to other elements

Na 11
Sodium

- Bonds with chlorine to make table salt
- Never found alone

Mg 12
Magnesium

- Necessary for plants and animals
- Found in sparklers

Al 13
Aluminum

- Used in airplanes for its weight and strength
- Used in foil, cables

Si 14
Silicon

- Found in sand, stone, and soil
- Used in computer chips

P 15
Phosphorus

- Used in matches, detergents, fertilizers
- Found in bones

S 16
Sulfur

- Found in matches, fireworks, egg yolks
- Creates air pollution

Cl 17
Chlorine

- Combines with hydrogen to digest food
- Used in swimming pools

Ar 18
Argon

- Found in light bulbs
- Does not react or bond with any other element

(continued on next page)

Element Go Fish

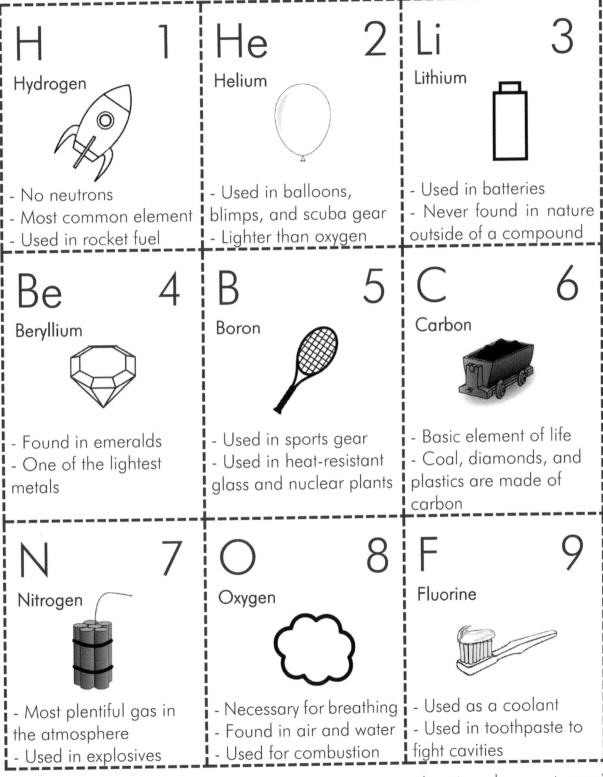

H 1

Hydrogen

- No neutrons
- Most common element
- Used in rocket fuel

He 2

Helium

- Used in balloons, blimps, and scuba gear
- Lighter than oxygen

Li 3

Lithium

- Used in batteries
- Never found in nature outside of a compound

Be 4

Beryllium

- Found in emeralds
- One of the lightest metals

B 5

Boron

- Used in sports gear
- Used in heat-resistant glass and nuclear plants

C 6

Carbon

- Basic element of life
- Coal, diamonds, and plastics are made of carbon

N 7

Nitrogen

- Most plentiful gas in the atmosphere
- Used in explosives

O 8

Oxygen

- Necessary for breathing
- Found in air and water
- Used for combustion

F 9

Fluorine

- Used as a coolant
- Used in toothpaste to fight cavities

(continued on next page)

Element Go Fish

Ne 10
Neon
OPEN

- Used in lights, lasers
- Never bonds to other elements

Na 11
Sodium

- Bonds with chlorine to make table salt
- Never found alone

Mg 12
Magnesium

- Necessary for plants and animals
- Found in sparklers

Al 13
Aluminum

- Used in airplanes for its weight and strength
- Used in foil, cables

Si 14
Silicon

- Found in sand, stone, and soil
- Used in computer chips

P 15
Phosphorus

- Used in matches, detergents, fertilizers
- Found in bones

S 16
Sulfur

- Found in matches, fireworks, egg yolks
- Creates air pollution

Cl 17
Chlorine

- Combines with hydrogen to digest food
- Used in swimming pools

Ar 18
Argon

- Found in light bulbs
- Does not react or bond with any other element

Experiment Worksheet

Fill out this worksheet as you work through the experiment.

Question: _____

Hypothesis: _____
_____

Materials: _____
_____

Procedure: _____
_____
_____
_____
_____

Observations/data: _____
_____
_____
_____

Conclusion: _____
_____
_____

Research Notes

Use these pages to make notes on your topic.

Topic:_____

Resource 1:_____

Info:_____   Info:_____

Info:_____   Info:_____

Info:_____   Info:_____

Resource 2:_____

Info:_____   Info:_____

Info:_____   Info:_____

Info:_____   Info:_____

Resource 3:_____

Info:_____   Info:_____

Info:_____   Info:_____

Info:_____   Info:_____

Resource 4:_____

Info:_____   Info:_____

Info:_____   Info:_____

Info:_____   Info:_____

Resource 5:_____

Info:_____   Info:_____

Info:_____   Info:_____

Info:_____   Info:_____

Resource 6:_____

Info:_____   Info:_____

Info:_____   Info:_____

Info:_____   Info:_____

Resource 7:_____

Info:_____   Info:_____

Info:_____   Info:_____

Info:_____   Info:_____

Resource 8:_____

Info:_____   Info:_____

Info:_____   Info:_____

Info:_____   Info:_____

Resource 9:_____

Info:_____   Info:_____

Info:_____   Info:_____

Info:_____   Info:_____

Science Report Checklist

Use this checklist to help you as you finish up your science project. Aim for a checkmark in each box.

Research
☐ Facts
☐ Sources
☐ Bibliography

Project
☐ 3D
☐ Neat
☐ Teaches all about your topic; shows off all you learned
☐ Self-explanatory: someone could look at it and understand what it's all about without you explaining it to them
☐ Bibliography displayed with project

Experiment
☐ Demonstrates your topic
☐ Neatly written up with all parts of the experiment worksheet
☐ Able to be done over and over with the same results

Demonstration
☐ Clearly state what your project is about
☐ Tell about what they will learn from your project
☐ Explain how the experiment relates to your topic
☐ Demonstrate the experiment
☐ State your conclusion
☐ Ask if anyone has questions

Made in the USA
Columbia, SC
08 August 2020